Regatta Lepa

Sea Gypsies

Here is our house.

Our house is on the water.

Here is our boat.

Our boat is on the water too.

Look at us!

We are playing on our boat.

We are fishing

from our boat.

We are with our family
on our boat.

I am with my friends
on our boat.

9

Our boat is special.

We put **decorations**

on our boat.

We put umbrellas and **flags** on our boat.

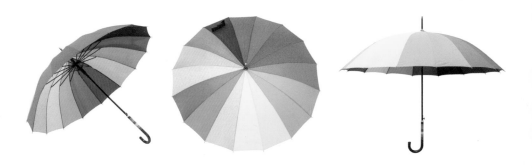

We put rugs and streamers on our boat.

Look at our boat now.

15

Glossary

decorations

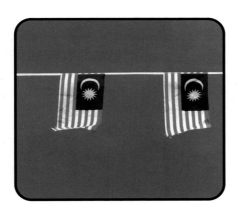

flags